Words of a Mute

A Dialogue with the Divine

by

Auden Ray

The Penman's Press

Words of a Mute

ISBN: 979-8-9998487-1-0
Published by The Penman's Press
First Edition

Printed in the United States of America

For Owen

This book was written for my son, Owen, and for the next generations to come. May these words draw them closer to God.

Foreword

This is a compilation of thoughts that arose involuntarily and without planning. For years, I have lived with disrupted sleep, and in those moments, these thoughts came to me as reassurance and revelation. As the world has largely silenced the words of our Lord, I am sharing these reflections so they may stand as a testimony of my faith. These were the words that accompanied me when life became difficult.

An Instrument

Maybe it is not the skill He wants me to show.

Maybe it is not the art He wants me to exhibit.

Maybe it is the words He wants me to reach.

Ultimately, it is the words that needed to be written.

I am not a penman. It is never my desire. My process is only a feeble attempt to follow my instinct in this life, so that I might witness the path to be with my Creator once more, because He has found me.

We are all stranded on this earth, passing through the beginning and the end of time. Knowing there was a beginning and an end, as we see it in the birth and the death of a star.

We do not know others' background but our own. Each of us is destined to do the things we are meant to do. Sometimes we found one, but we were not aware. Sometimes it was already given to us, but we did not like it and wanted something else.

What if the earth we are on is already the Garden of Eden?

Whether through science, psychology, philosophy, art, or music, every aspects of life leads back to the same origin.

The value of doing is not about being the best among others; but it is about how happy one is while doing.

By simply existing, we have already glorified God.

After all, two thousand and twenty-five years have passed. Time has muffled His Words, and the world has drifted away from them.

He has shown us His Kingdom in many ways. He brought all of us the salvation, whether we recognize Him or not. If the world we live in is not just a world, but in fact the Garden of Eden, have we truly found it?

The thing that we want most is the thing we need to lose most.

We see differently because our brains are different.

What the eyes cannot see, the heart can. The Kingdom is for the heart to discover, not the eyes. Everything we see in this world we cannot take to Heaven. We know we exist in this world through our five senses

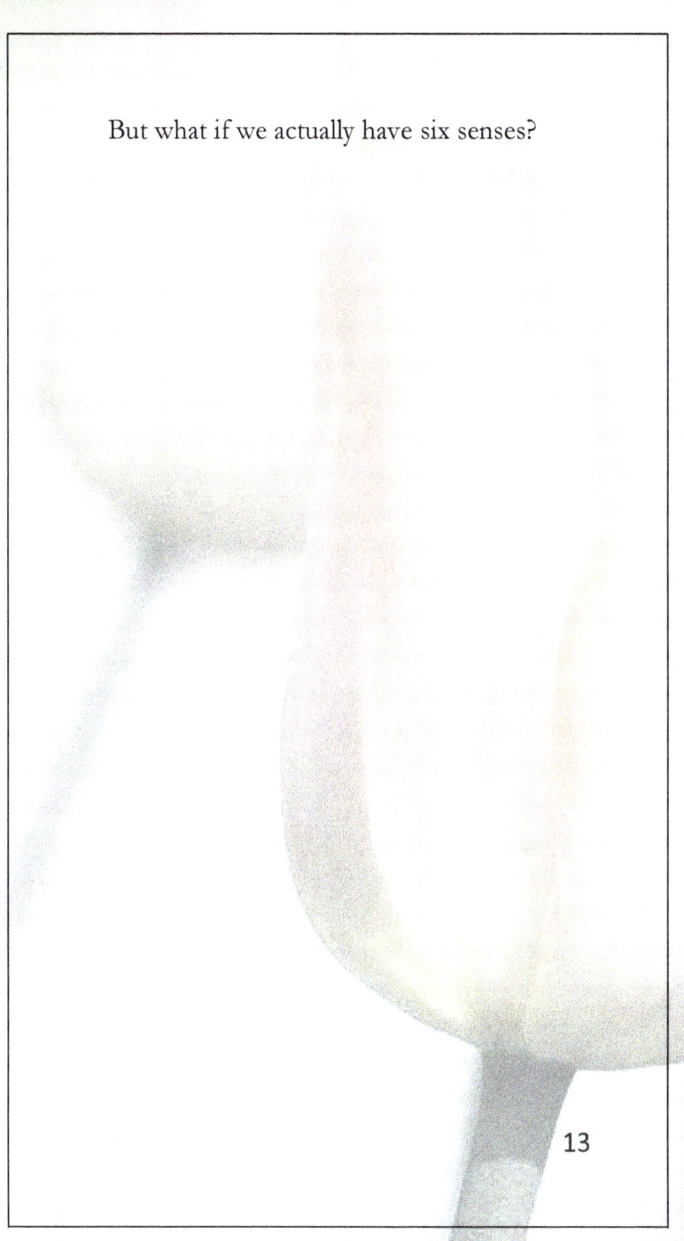

But what if we actually have six senses?

If our brain is not present, we will not know we are truly present in this world.

No person is alike, just as no fingerprint is alike. We were designed to be uniquely created, and this manifests as our individual character. Avoid adopting the world's standard of character. Create your own.

One must cultivate the soul more than anything as we are mostly caught up in surviving in this world. However, survival itself only lasts for a short while.

I share my fear, the fear of missing something. But He said: "What if the missing is needed so that I may fill it in?"

What if the isolation is to shield me from the great flood, like in Noah's ark?

We often dwell within our memories. Memories are an ocean of thoughts and emotions. It appears as clear as water when we begin to reflect on the past. When we have included Him as part of our lives, we eventually discover the meaning of our experiences. Only in the bad times is He calling us, and we are able to respond to his calling because we simply start listening. Though we think he is absent, he is always present. We are all destined to live in the image of God.

We are always drawn to the things we need most. We don't know why, but slowly we come to understand that it is part of a healing process. There are many remedies offered in this world to combat suffering, but they are merely bandages. How often do we rest our hearts in Him? When are we going to pick up our cross and walk? As we understand His suffering, we also understand ours.

We shall care for all that God has entrusted to us, whether in the realm of matter or in the realm of the mind. For it is within the mind that the Kingdom of God resides. And from the mind, the realm of matter is transformed.

When one is close to God, the devil could not bear it, but must depart.

In a world full of division, the dark force is gaining ground. The only way to counter that is to unify. As the Gospel teaches: "If you love your enemy, you will have no enemy."

We are mirrors, reflecting the light. The words are the light.

It is through suffering that our hearts can be opened.

"All animals are Christians," said my little boy.

If you are not thankful, many good chances
and opportunities will slip away.

We have lived in a society that is becoming less and less free. But the worst is when we get accustomed to it.

God is the humblest, as He never reveals Himself, but only to be reflected in His creation.

We live our lives fullest based on the will of God. When we live by His will, then our lives have become the fullest.

Many people cannot find God, though God is in the very place they are at.

They tend to keep searching for God by changing location, or pursuing things that induce slight and short-lived happiness.

People are often seeing what others have, but not what others do not have. They are often seeing what they do not have, but not what they have.

People tend to get close to those who are materially blessed. But it is the neglected ones who need more care. Work for God, find them.

Believe comes first, then ask, seek, and you will find.

Nothing is more precious than being alone with contentment.

What is the purpose and function of pain? It is through pain that we are drawn close to God and it is through pain that we truly rely on him. It is through pain when we are once again found.

If we do not open the door to imagination, how can God inspire you?

When you deal with difficulties, talk to God and ask him for help as a friend. He will grant you the determination to say, "I will do it"

Why do strong and weak people mingle together?

One person might argue: “I am in a condition that compels me to be strong, because everyone around me is weak.” Conversely, the weaker person might respond: “I am weak because I being taken care of by someone strong. God then concludes and says: “it is destined to be that so that you both can compensate each other as man is not meant to live alone.”

The medicine of love and then the desire to love are, by design, a natural formula given by God. He wants us to reproduce. He started by creating the conditions, or the environment, which involved numerous tests and failures. Yet, he persevered. He then made the first life form to serve as an experiment, and continued this work by creating other life forms. After he made the last one, he stopped. We are the last.

God gives us puzzles to solve. He is happy when we solve them.

The law of life is governed by God.

If you cannot find God anywhere, search for whatever goodness you can find; that is where He lies. You will soon find yourself drawn to where He is until eventually, you see Him everywhere. He is nowhere, and yet, He is everywhere.

Our bodies are clothes for our souls.

Light does not need to go to the light; light only has most of the effect in shining through dark places. Spread the goodness to the people who really need it.

When we talk to God in our hearts, we know he listens, because he lives there.

By distancing ourselves from the crowd, we see through everything. But when we see things with the crowd, we gain a company.

The wild flower has no roots,

The wind blows wherever it pleases.

It blows wherever He pleases.

We are the same in the eyes of God.

If you find something difficult to do, do it for God.

There are the two things that can save a country. The change does not come from the President, or any politics. It comes from a strong family unit and education.

We often let go of our children too soon. Birds do not abandon their young when they are learning to fly; the parents watch over their training. Yet humans care for their children least. They are not ready to live on their own or make every decision, but still, we release them too early. And when children do not reflect their parents' likings, they are pushed further away.

A good king listens to a good adviser.

The ones who are suppressed are precious in His eyes. Those who are not affected by worldly matters are the ones who find comfort only in Him.

The will of God is written all over each of us. We need only to discern where and what.

Be unafraid.

The token to heaven is not the coins we gather.

Words can heal; words can kill.

When our heart is at peace, God dwells within. We must prepare the condition for Him to remain Empty often our vessels so that the inspiration of God never ends.

We remain awake, for we never know when He will call.

We stay focused while we are awake, until the time we close our eyes in sleep.

Learn by God.

Learn from God.

Let God be our only teacher.

For those who already have a lot but still want more, they are the poorest.

Every labor is blessed. God has promised that in every situation, and no matter how dark it is, a kingdom of God can be placed in.

My freedom lives on the paper, in the realm of sound, and within my thoughts. Yet these stand in a stark contrast to the physical situation I am in. One can live by mere words. A bird once knew how to fly, but when kept in a cage too long, its wings stop working.

Nowadays, even evil cannot be disguised to appear good.

Sometimes, I talk to God as though He were beside me, and I sense His presence. Sometimes, He speaks.

Jesus looked over the lost sheep. He gathered more, and then more. He did not need force; the sheep recognized their Shepherd and went to Him.

Whoever hungers for power cannot hold power.

Let me be the vessel of God.

Bad voices accompany anger, therefore, do not be angry.

God wants me to speak of Him, so I do. And when I speak of Him, my heart flutters.

Nothing dies until its purpose is accomplished. Therefore, do not die without one.

In a world where people are so busy drawing attention to themselves, why not pay attention to God instead?

Instinct is drawn toward that which cannot be described.

God and Jesus are inseparable.

Happiness in the realm of the world,
without knowing God, lies in danger.

Be born again.

We are not commanded to love God; we are inspired to love Him.

True art does not need success to uphold it; if you truly love it, it has a place in your heart and it will reflect.

Art is not defined by public recognition. It is something purely private.

The joy of success is great, but the desire to create has surpassed all the enjoyment.

The heart and brain work together as a team. When the heart desires, the brain plansout a pathway.

Some endure physical pain, and others, mental torment. May they find peace in God's cure. He is the cure. Find Him.

Doing the will of God is very simple. Look at the world around you and sprinkle God's light here and there.

Be yourself and let God guide you through.

Pleasure makes the heart empty.

I work for God. It is my full-time job.

Me: Sorry son, I am not sure if I am doing the right thing for you to be successful one day because I myself am not successful.

Son: You are successful because you have an awesome son.

We rely on the companionship of God, for human reliance is but shifting sand.

Success is not a sudden explosion. But a slow growth. It is found in the small, faithful steps of a well-lived day.

God gave me gifts I did not know I had,
and I kept searching.

We do not need to feel important; we need to feel unimportant.

Your task is to make the most out of the worst situation.

Whenever there is goodness, God remains.

Be the vessels for God; be ready to fulfill His will. Even nature listens to Him.

Without competing, one can still triumph.

Money is but a token on earth; in God's kingdom, it has no value.

Human commitment is imperfect, but loyalty is a gift from God.

There was a time when I had to step away from my piano. Yet I still practiced regularly, because a gift given by God must be cared for. Now I know that my whole being needs it. It is part of me.

Unspoken words are gold written on paper.

When you do not fight, the battle is won instantly.

When my soul meets yours, our spirits find each other.

In the hut, I meet my Lord. In the palace, I do not. Therefore, I rather stay in the hut.

May our lives become the work of God.

When I stay in the house of God, everyone wants to come in.

Indeed, success brings happiness, but happiness cannot rely on success alone.

It is not about success or fortunes; it is about the place where I met my Lord.

When we finally become better humans, we will notice God noticing us.

Do not be a romantic lover; be a responsible and kind man; be one who can bear the weight of life.

We must not see ourselves through the perspectives of others; that is a haunting idea.

If you find the best of yourself, you will never have competition.

Words are thoughts and sound. They carry energy and frequency.

Yearn for the things that feed the soul, not the flesh.

Find the best of what can be done, and do it.

At the end of the day, I thought I was giving myself credit for handling my troubles well. But then I realized it was, in fact, all taken care of by God.

Sometimes it is not just about creating. You have to put a mastermind behind it.

The road to perfection is full of imperfections.

The road to heaven depends on how well we walk alone on our path.

Do not marry if your family of your birth is not cared for.

When we can absorb the pain of others, even though the pain is not our own, we finally begin to understand the true meaning of compassion.

Our salvation happens in the present.

Jesus told Peter to catch men. This is what we are called to do, so that not a single one would be lost. Some do it through inspiring. Some do it through charity, but some do the work of God through those they are closest to.

Some follow the masters to be the best.
Some find the flaws of the masters to be the best.

God plans everything for us; we just need to acknowledge that. Everything happening around us is perfectly calculated.

That unsettling side of you can only be resolved by God.

Everything happening to us is planned by God. Our only task is to discover His purpose in the work He is doing through us.

To others, they may not seem valuable; but to God, He has made you his best tool.

In the seen world we live in, we are only travelers. Be aware of the unseen world from which we originated, for one day we will return.

When you mourn for others, you forget the real reason to mourn.

My life journey does not lead to anywhere else; it only leads back to Him.

When you have found a purpose set by God, it means He has sent you. It also means that when your purpose is complete, you will return to Him.

Quit dreaming, open your eyes and see.

When I ponder deep enough, I have found my place.

If I have to help someone, how far am I willing to go?

When you decide not to follow others, you become your own master.

When I faced something difficult, I prayed deeply to God, asking Him to show me a way, or a solution. And He always helped.

When I thought he had abandoned me, that was the time he sculpted a better me. That was the time something incredible was transforming within me.

Be kind to the one who you think they have wronged you. Because what we are going to do to them may cause a wound deeper than the wrong itself.

We do not need the perfect condition to strive when we are with God.

Seeing God will always make you beautiful.

In this world, it is not about luck. It is about how well you find a solution and how swiftly you act upon it.

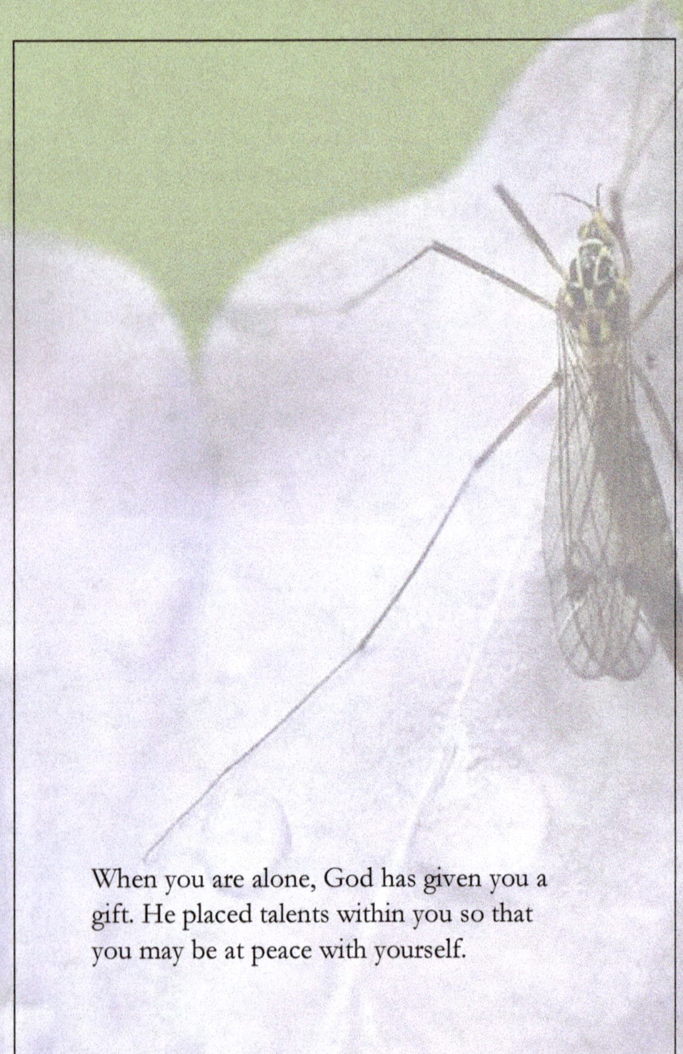

When you are alone, God has given you a gift. He placed talents within you so that you may be at peace with yourself.

If you want to escape, the only world you want to escape to is the world of God.

My son often drew close to me, guiding me on what not to say. He told me, "Act normal and you will be fine." Then he stood up, accepting the fault as his own, so that I would not bear the blame.

It is when we are at the lowest point where we are reborn.

These are some undesiring characteristics a person has. Watch for signs when they are demanding, petty, unforgiving, unable to handle stress well, forceful, etc. Stay away from them if you get to know them. Because once they become your spouse, your children will have to deal with them while growing up. Avoid also someone who has a very strong possession sense and who could not let go on things.

Never marry a person you cannot know well enough his or her character. Because not only that you sign a bad contract, your children will have to grow up dealing with this problem. However, if you do, make the best out of the worst situation.

Marry someone your parents would approve.

Opportunity does not come easily. When it appears, make the most of it.

What happens on the outside does not matter. What happens in the inside does.

People who are getting old must simplify their lives.

If plants were to sin, they would want to be animals. They would not want to live and grow. They would not want to save all their energy for the offspring.

Healing will come from a person who holds the peace.

When those who do good deeds are spent by the unthankful, God will call his faithful home. And the unthankful will be left to walk through their own trials.

She is almost perfect, but God gives her a flaw so that others may learn to accept her.

When a goal of an achievement is praise from others, we will never know that it is God who is pleased first before anyone else.

I have many positive thoughts, and I need to write them all down.

When all around me fall into sin, I can be the one who does not.

I can be in the midst of a very bad situation,
but I do not fall.

We learn from the poor, poor in wealth, poor in knowledge, poor in spirit.

When you are persecuted and mocked, your divine shield is up.

A prisoner's imagination has surpassed the freeman.

While people want God to make something happen to them, I would rather find out what I can do for God. God needs us to make something happen for Him.

Some men should be monks; they do not know God is waiting for them.

Do not rely on how others see you, but how you see from within. But most importantly, rely on how God sees you.

If you are becoming an artist, you must be very careful whom you marry. If your daughter is an artist, you must advise her and teach her to be selective. Otherwise, she will be buried. For artists need support. Will you provide your daughter with unlimited support?

Some people know God by obeying the rules, some know God when they end up in prison.

When we are learning the complexity of science, we witness the mystery of God's love for us.

The most entertaining is not a thing, but a thought.

Happiness should be internal. If not, it will only lead to more unhappiness. The only eternal happiness is through God alone.

We have lost the ability to connect to God directly in this world. Only if we can find God's realm, we will always have that connection.

www.ingramcontent.com/pod-product-compliance
Lightning Source LLC
La Vergne TN
LVHW010902110826
845149LV00005B/1449

* 9 7 9 8 9 9 9 8 4 8 7 1 0 *